Boko Haram: The History of Africa's Most

By Charles River Ed

A picture of Abubakar Shekau, the leader of Boko Haram, in late 2014

About Charles River Editors

Charles River Editors provides superior editing and original writing services across the digital publishing industry, with the expertise to create digital content for publishers across a vast range of subject matter. In addition to providing original digital content for third party publishers, we also republish civilization's greatest literary works, bringing them to new generations of readers via ebooks.

Sign up here to receive updates about free books as we publish them, and visit Our Kindle Author Page to browse today's free promotions and our most recently published Kindle titles.

Introduction

The First Lady holding a sign in reference to Boko Haram's kidnapping of Nigerian schoolgirls

Boko Haram

"Boko Haram are better armed and are better motivated than our own troops. Given the present state of affairs, it is absolutely impossible for us to defeat Boko Haram." - Kashim Shettima, governor of Borno

On the morning of April 15, 2004, the world woke up to the extraordinary news of the kidnap in a little known hamlet of Nigeria of some 276, primarily Christian schoolgirls, by the radical militant Nigerian insurgent group Boko Haram. Almost overnight, the group, which had resided somewhat on the fringes of global consciousness up until that point, found itself at the forefront as international public outrage, culminating in a social media campaign headed by First Lady Michelle Obama, demanded the immediate return of the kidnapped girls.

Those demands, while laudable, simply served to project a hitherto local and regional jihadist movement, operating in the gray hinterland of the African Sahel region, into an organization with an international profile and a place in the pantheon of globally recognized terror organizations. If anything, the headlines have probably imbued Boko Haram with more punch than it can practically wield, for in reality the organization, at least for the time being, it remains less a jihadist movement that a localized terror insurgency with very locally defined objectives. If Boko

Haram does indeed nurture international ambitions, which increasingly it appears to, then these perhaps are a fringe expression of a movement that appears in on the whole, again at least for the time being, to be too haphazard, and chaotic in its administration and leadership to really find a home amongst the larger and better known international organizations.

Boko Haram: The History of Africa's Most Notorious Terrorist Group looks at the history that led to the rise of Boko Haram, and a glimpse of what the future may hold. Along with pictures of important people, places, and events, you will learn about Boko Haram like never before, in no time at all.

Boko Haram: The History of Africa's Most Notorious Terrorist Group

About Charles River Editors

Introduction

Chapter 1: The Historic Social Divide in Nigeria

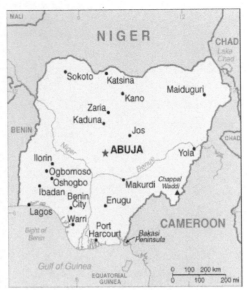

A map of Nigeria

The modern state of Nigeria, as it is recognizable today, came into being in 1914, with the creation of the British *Colony and Protectorate of Nigeria*. This was the defining moment when the vaunted British theory of *Indirect Rule* found practical expression, and the point at which the idealism of a handful of enlightened British colonial civil servants was put to the test.

The early evolution of Nigeria as a British overseas territory had followed a somewhat formularized pattern that by the end of the 19th century had been established in the wider empire, but perhaps most particularly in Africa.

In the British African context there existed fundamentally two systems of colonial rule. The first of these tended to concern those territories that offered opportunity for permanent and large scale European habitation and the second being those that did not. In this regard, South Africa was obviously recognized as the flagship British territory in Africa. It was potentially the wealthiest, it was the most strategically located in regards to British maritime interests, but, perhaps most importantly, it was climatically suitable for extensive white settlement, which, to a lesser extent was true for other British African possessions, such as Southern and Northern Rhodesia (Zimbabwe/Zambia), Nyasaland (Malawi) and Kenya.

However, there were also those territories that did not naturally lend themselves to the European temper, all of which tended to be located within the deep tropics of the continent where a combination of climate and disease rendered expatriate settlement at the very least uncomfortable and in some cases deadly. These territories were on the whole penetrated initially by Christian missionaries, acting under the impetus of faith, and arriving on the coast in the aftermath of early European maritime trading interests. The missionaries were in due course followed by the early geographic explorers, before finally both yielded to private capital interests in the form of Royal Chartered Companies, which would usually in turn be the precursor to formal colonial annexation. This last phase of African colonial expansion in Africa took place through the latter phases of the 19th century.

So in terms of the British purview at least, West Africa fell very much into the commercial and strategic fields of endeavour, with perhaps the greatest motivation for British expansion in the region being in response to concurrent French expansion.[1] And it was this, in fact, that was the basis upon which a royal charter was granted to the *Royal Niger Company*, founded by the great Victorian capitalist, Sir George Taubman Goldie; ostensibly to provide an organized bulwark against French commercial interests that were beginning to impinge on what had hitherto been a rather haphazard and disorganized British commercial dominance of the Niger delta region.

It is perhaps also worth pointing out here that the modern history of the west African region as a whole, in particular in relation to the activities of all its various European interlopers, tended to be informed in large part by the Atlantic Slave Trade, which, of course, coincided with the development and industrialization of the plantation economies of the Americas. During this period European involvement in West Africa consisted of little more than highly organized plunder, which, although lucrative, was also manifestly unsustainable. Towards the middle of the 1800s, therefore, the complexion of business in the region necessarily began to alter, in particular in the aftermath of British abolition, from which point a tendency towards more infrastructure dependent and sustainable systems of commerce required a far greater degree of organization, management and security. This was provided by the *Royal Niger Company* in exchange for extremely liberal trading rights and a more or less free hand in pacifying and establishing a basic system of European administration in the region.

As a consequence, when the Berlin Conference of 1884/85 was convened in order to map out European spheres of influence in Africa, and thereafter to set in motion the greatest land grab in human history, *The Scramble for Africa*, Britain was in a position, thanks largely to the efforts of Sir George Taubman Goldie, to claim the Niger delta region and its hinterland as a British sphere of influence. This preceded annexation of the territory, along with quite a large swath of what was at that time still referred to on international shipping charts as the *Slave Coast*.

Thus, with an imprimatur in hand to pacify and govern, legalized by its royal charter, the *Royal Niger Company* established a firm British presence in the region, and the era of modern Nigeria was born. At that point the coast and the northern reaches of the territory were declared separate British protectorates under Company administration, with the British imperial government itself only assuming control of the combined Niger territories in 1900. Then, in 1914, the two protectorates merged to form the *Colony and Protectorate of Nigeria*.

The logic of retaining two separate British protectorates under separate colonial administrations had been in respect of the clear social delineation between the north and the south of what would in due course become the territory of Nigeria. Broadly speaking, the

---

[1] Note: French colonial expansion in the region proceeded under not dissimilar impetus to the British and German, but in the aftermath of the loss of the first French empire, and France's defeat in the Franco/Prussian War of 1871, France tended to be more acutely conscious of prestige in her quest for imperial expansion globally, but in particular in Africa.

territory could be divided evenly between the Christian/animist south and the Islamic north, which early colonial bureaucrats recognized as not only a cultural, but also an administrative fault line. It is also fair to say that key members of the British administration at the time, led by arguably one of the most enlightened colonial civil servants of his age, Sir Frederick Lugard, tended to have something of an exaggerated regard for native aristocracies, and the ancient, pious and scholarly aristocracies of the Islamic north of Nigeria conformed very much to this pattern.

Although there are hundreds of languages spoken in modern Nigeria, there are seven of these that dominate, and they are *Hausa, Igbo, Yoruba, Ibibio, Edo, Fulfulde*, and *Kanuri*. Among these the three principal regional languages are *Hausa, Yoruba* and *Igbo*, spoken respectively by ethnic groupings of the same name. In very general terms, the Hausa/Fulani group dominate the regions north of the Benue/Niger river confluence, and the Yoruba/Igbo group predominate in the south. The Yoruba occupy the territories west of the Niger River and the Igbo those to the east, bordering Cameroon. The Yoruba and Igbo share the single commonality of not being Muslim, which created the essential and largely irreconcilable fault line that the British found existing between the north and south of future Nigeria.

Picture of the border with Cameroon

When encountered by early colonial administrators, however, the general perception tended to be that the sultanates and emirates of the north represented the African native at his finest. It would here be instructive perhaps to quote from a London times editorial of 1904, written by Edwardian journalist and social commentator Flora Shaw, who also happened to be the wife of Lord Lugard: "The Fulani were a striking people, dark in complexion, but of the distinguished features, small hands, and fine, rather aristocratic, carriage of the Arabs on the Mediterranean coast. They were of the Mahomedan (sic) religion, and were held by those who knew them to be naturally endowed with the characteristics which fitted them for rule. Their theory of justice was good, though their practice was bad; their scheme of taxation was most elaborate and was carried even into a system of death duties which left little for an English Chancellor of the Exchequer to improve."[2]

It was this rather sycophantic regard that set the tone for the British policy of *Indirect Rule* as it applied to territories like Nigeria. In its simplest from, Indirect Rule, which was a concept conceived and implement by Lord Frederick Lugard himself, implied the devolution of all the day-to-day administrative responsibilities of government to the pre-existing traditional authority, with imperial superintendentship visible only at the center, and existing at all times within an advisory capacity. A natural corollary of this policy would be to ensure the modernization of tradition systems of government, law, tax collection and justice with the understanding that at some point they would emerge with not only their traditional identities intact, but also compatible with modern systems of government.

And in this regard, the Islamic north of Nigeria, with its long established and relatively sophisticated traditions of centralized authority, offered a perfect template. Not so the comparatively chaotic and primitive south, darker in complexion, more decentralized and disordered in their social organization, and politically fractured and individualistic. This is what Lord Lugard had to say about the Igbo, the largest ethnic group in eastern Nigeria, and arguably the most decentralized of all the tribes of the territory. "The great Ibo [Igbo] race to the East of the Niger, numbering some 3 millions, and their cognate tribes had not developed beyond the stage of primitive savagery."[3]

These were uncharitable words indeed, but forgivable perhaps at a time immediately after the devastation of the slave trade, and before the general proliferation of Christian missionary influence and English education in the region. However, at the moment that these influences did begin to be felt in the Protectorate as a whole, it was the southern groupings, and particularly the Igbo, who embraced and absorbed the enormous advantages and potentialities that were offered by the modern world.

Conversely, the more conservative elements in the north, bound by their disdain of modern education, their resistance to Christianity and their adherence to increasingly archaic social and political conventions, began ever more to slip into an anachronistic, and indeed atavistic state of mind, maintaining their aristocratic expectations, protected as they were by the British, while at the same time yielding an ever increasing responsibility for administration and business to the educated and ambitious elements from the south, primarily the Igbo. Soon the Igbo in particular began to form large and thriving expatriate pockets in the north that daily challenged the relevance of these ancient aristocracies, breeding considerable resentment against the black south, which was, of course, an impotent resentment so long as the British remained in ultimate control.

With the grant of independence from Britain in October 1960, however, and not withstanding extraordinarily diligent efforts on the part of the British to groom Nigeria for independence, the degree and depth of ethnic tension within the colony had been grotesquely underestimated, and

[2] Times (London). *Lady Lugard on Nigeria.* March 2, 1904, p. 12
[3] Quoted: Arinze, Josh. *Moral Anguish: Richard Nixon and the Challenge of Biafra.* Kindle Edition.

within five years of Britain relinquishing the territory, a boiling pot of internal contradiction erupted in a series of military coups, ethnic pogroms and ultimately civil war.

The dynamics of the Nigerian Civil War, or the Biafran War, are perhaps superficial to this narrative, it is important to understand it to the extent that it sheds light on the north/south divide in Nigeria. The essential element that triggered a war of succession in Nigeria was a series of violent, indeed perhaps even genocidal pogroms that were unleashed against Igbo expatriate communities, primarily in northern Nigeria, and Igbo elements within the military, in both cases in the immediate aftermath of two military coups that took place during 1966. Much of this had to do with general resentment against the Igbo for their apparent success and dominance in the immediate post-independence period, precipitating a move towards succession in eastern Nigeria that culminated in declared independence and the creation of the state of Biafra in the territory east of the Niger River.

The conflict was resolved in 1970 with the ultimate defeat of Biafra and the reunification of Nigeria, but lingering ethnic tensions continued to exist across religious and ethnic lines, exacerbated by the perpetuation of military rule long after the conclusion of the civil war, resulting in blatant abuses of power and ever deepening economic and political corruption, the latter in particular in terms of natural resources, with oil wealth being the most notable example, and, of course, the multiple cross currents of political patronage that naturally followed. All of this resulted in a grotesquely unbalanced distribution of wealth, widespread poverty and a great deal of burgeoning political discontent, all of which offered fertile ground for a weakening of the centre and a proliferation of lawlessness, ultimately, and almost inevitably, manifesting in an armed insurgency.

The green parts of Nigeria currently operate under sharia law.

Chapter 2: The Rise of Boko Haram

The roots of Boko Haram can be found in the same fertile soil of many other spontaneous regional and continental African rebel and insurgent organizations, that being weak an ineffective central government, political patronage, tribalism, regionalism, unequal distribution of land resources and of course that great and most debilitating factor in African political and economic life: corruption. And moreover, it is perhaps fair to say that the religious overtones of the Boko Haram ideology, if such can be described, tends to have less to do with international jihadism than the demographic peculiarities of Nigeria as it was returned to the continent by the British.

In quite the same way as such perennial regions of instability as the Central African remain locked in conflict thanks to the arbitrary frontier delineations of the colonial era, so the fundamentally irreconcilable differences between the Islamic north of Africa and the Christian/animist south will continue to ferment animosity and unrest in the region, as witnessed in South Sudan, Darfur and of course, more recently, in Nigeria itself.[4]

From the somewhat protected ascendency of the colonial and immediate post-colonial period, the Islamic north of Nigeria began after independence to fall increasingly behind in terms of access to wealth and political capital to the more aggressively modern south. The system of federalism that the British established prior to independence was for the most part configured to satisfy northern demands for as loose as possible a political union in order to preserve the Islamic identity of the north.[5] A separate system of justice was permitted in the north in order to accommodate Sharia as a personal status law, while the northern religious and political leader, Sir Amadu Bello, presided over a virtually autonomous administrative system.

---

[4] Note: this, of course, does not preclude tensions within the Islamic north itself, with different ethnic groups practicing Islam in different ways, and with tribal and ethnic differences often proving to be stronger than religious similarities.

[5] Note: the original Federation of Nigeria was defined by three states, North, West and East, with Lagos existing as a separate administrative district.

Bello

While this sense of inevitably autonomy fell away in the aftermath of the 1966 coups, followed by the advent of military rule, adherence to Islam, and a strong sense of separate identity, remained a powerful factor in the north.[6] Sir Amadu Bello was one of the first high profile victims of the first 1966 coup, after which the north fell under the secular rule of the military. As a consequence throughout the 1970s and 1980s a number of Islamic pressure groups began to emerge, most notable amongst them *Izala*, which was active in the late 1970s, and which called for a return to the fundamentals of Islam, followed by the *Muslim Brothers*, who, in the 1980s, were active under the slogan: '*There is no Government but Islam.*'[7]

These, however, were for the most part moderate pressure groups acting broadly speaking peacefully, and within the law, but the seeds of radical Islam also existed at the same time, with perhaps the most notable militant organization in existence at that time being the *Yan Tatsine* movement, under the messianic leadership of a radical cleric by the name of Muhammadu Marwa, or Maitatsine Hausa – *He Who Curses* – who led the first violent demonstrations in the Kano state of northern Nigeria in protest at growing corruption under military rule, and the increasing political and economic marginalization of the north.

---

[6] Note: Pressure in the south for a more unitary system of government tended to be realized with the advent of military rule, which corresponded to the centralized command structure of the military and its tendency to respond to a strong central command.

[7] *Boko Haram and the Nigerian Insurgency [Kindle Edition]* Brendan McNamara (Author, Editor), Ryan Milliken (Author), Allen Chatt (Author), Evan Procknow (Author), Graham Plaster (Editor) *The Intelligence Community LLC*

A picture of Kano, Nigeria's biggest city

These sentiments did not ease with a return to democracy in Nigeria 1999, and the emergence of southern Christian Olusegun Obasanjo as the first democratically elected president of the country since the 1966 coups.[8] Islamic groups in the north soon afterwards attempted to assert a somewhat separatist agenda by adopting Sharia law in twelve northern states; although in fairness a certain amount of cautious moderation accompanied the practical implementation of Sharia.

---

[8] Note: Obasanjo served as a military leader of Nigeria between 1976 and 1979.

Obasanjo

This, therefore, is the soil within which the seeds of Boko Haram began to germinate. From the multiple threads of Islamic discontent under the corrupt and at times arbitrary rule of the federal government, the Boko Haram movement began to coalesce, anonymously at first, with no clear point traceable to determine its actual founding.

Most scholars, however, are in agreement that the first identifiable root of the organization was a loose grouping of Muslim scholars who met in 1995 under the name of *Ahlulsunna wai'jama'ah hijra*, led by Islamic scholar Abubaker Lawan, and comprising for the most part a cabal of moderate, middle aged and middle class men interested primarily in the study of orthodox Islam.

Change in the organization, however, coincided more or less with democratization in Nigeria. Lawan left the country to study at the University of Medina in Saudi Arabia, relinquishing leadership of the organization to a younger and more radicalized Muslim scholar by the name of Mohammed Yusuf. Yusuf could claim only sparse formal education, but a great deal of revolutionary zeal that had been honed through a radical Quranic indoctrination acquired in neighboring Chad and Niger.[9] From Yusuf a strong militant message emerged, decrying the dilution of orthodox Islam under the influence of the political and economic patronage. This message was characterized by strong and defiant sermons that began to influence the

---

[9] It is interesting to note that in interviews before his death, Mohammed Yusuf told the BBC Hausa Service he believed the earth was flat, and that rain was not caused by evaporation from the ground, leading to a general sense of public derision towards the group, and a tendency to not take it seriously enough to examine its aims.

organization, creating out of it something of a movement dominated by a single charismatic leader, followed by a withdrawal from mainstream society in order to explore a utopian version of religious life under the undiluted tenets of orthodox Islam.

Yusuf

Part of this reversionism was a complete rejection of western style education, which caused those more moderate elements within society to refer to the organization as *Boko Haram*. This, in the idiomatic form of the Hausa language, implies something to the effect of *western education is forbidden*, but literally means book, or *boko*, unlawful, or *haram*. The organization itself eschewed this name, and indeed to an extent it still does, preferring the more formal name Jamā'at Ahl as-Sunnah lid-Da'wah wa'l-Jihād, or *Group of the People of Sunnah for Preaching and Jihad*.

Under Yusuf, the moderate elements of the movement drifted away, being replaced by an increasingly radical membership pursuing a more vociferous and militant agenda. This message proved to have considerable resonance, and despite a certain amount of localized disquiet, Boko Haram began to attract membership from among a wide spectrum of northern Nigerians – from impoverished inner city youth to university students – and attracting support from a variety of influential sources. Mohammed Yusuf established a mosque in the Borno State capital of Maidiguri, there offering a radical if somewhat ad hoc Quranic education to all comers, which added to an already dedicated radical base.

These educational activities appeared through the early part of the new decade to occupy the energies of the group, with only sporadic clashes with police and security agencies being recorded, and generally not attracting much attention. This remained the case until about 2008/9, at which point major clashes between the group and security authorities began to generate wider popular support, culminating in major riots in 2009 after state security agents raided a Boko Haram hideout, triggering days of social unrest.

This particular episode was significant for many reasons. In the first instance, obviously, it served clear notice to any who cared to listen of the scope of popular discontent in the north, but it also elevated Boko Haram to the status of a major national security risk. However, perhaps most importantly, it resulted in the detention and extra-judicial killing of Muhammad Yusuf by police, which created the movement's first martyr, opening the way for the ascension to the leadership of Yusuf's deputy, a man by the name of Abubakar Shekau.[10]

This manifestly unstable character completed the evolution of Boko Haram from a minor thorn in the side of the Nigerian Security Services to the status of full blown insurgency, and an organization that attracted not only the attention, but also the concern of the United States, which was, of course, precisely the credential that Abubakar Shekau and many at the leadership of the organization desired.

Abubakar Shekau

Chapter 3: Boko Haram's Military Capability

Religious disturbances have been a feature of the social landscape of northern Nigeria since the

---

[10] Note: Abubakar Shekau is also known by the alias of *Darul Akeem wa Zamunda Tawheed*, or *Darul Tawheed*, meaning in both instance *the home of monotheism.*

establishment of the Sokoto Caliphate in 1809, and thereafter sporadically throughout the phases of colonial and military rule. However, it was not until the advent of democracy in the country, and the attempt to establish Sharia Law in Kaduna State, that deadly sectarian violence flared up throughout the northern region, to the extent that it has by now become almost commonplace.

It is generally accepted, however, that Boko Haram as a militant organization did not appear as an actor in this ongoing religious turmoil until July of 2009, at which point a relatively innocuous incident involving the group catalyzed weeks of unprecedented violence that ran across several restive northern states.

There are a number of different versions in circulation regarding precisely what took place, but the most credible is simply that a group of Boko Haram members and supporters, travelling in a convoy to a funeral in the Borno State capital of Maiduguri, were stopped at a police roadblock outside the city where it was insisted that they adhere to a local law requiring the use of motorcycle crash helmets. This prompted an argument that resulted eventually in a gunfight, ending in the deaths of a number of Boko Haram members.[11] This episode immediately triggered a massive escalation of religious riots and violence that very quickly spread to Kano, Yobe and Borno, beginning a domino effect of violence and counter violence that saw Boko Haram's coming out as a fully constituted armed insurgency.

Equipped with hand grenades and small arms, groups of Boko Haram fighters took to the streets, attacking a police station in the city of Bauchi, which resulted in the deaths of between 32 and 39 militants, along with an undisclosed number of police and soldiers. At the same time, police stations in the cities of Potiskum and Wudil were also targeted, with sporadic gun battles then breaking out in various other locations, resulting in probably a preponderance of Boko Haram deaths, but also killing a significant number of police and security personnel.

The violence was eventually contained, but the episode considerably unnerved the federal authorities, although local public and press pronouncements tended to claim that the violence had been preempted by authorities, and that, had it not been, events might well have been significantly worse.

Then, on July 28, 2009, police surrounded the home of Ustaz Mohammad Yusuf's parents-in-law – although other reports state that Yusuf was located at a Boko Haram compound in Maiduguri – where Yusuf himself was arrested and taken into custody, and soon afterwards killed.

Again, there is a great deal of confusion over the exact sequence of events leading up to his death, but it is broadly accepted that, having escaped from police custody, Yusuf was quickly re-detained by security force elements and handed back over to the police, who, on the morning of July 30, 2009, publically executed him in the ground of the police station.

The events of July 26-30, 2009 are now broadly referred to as the *2009 Boko Haram Uprising*, marking more or less the point at which the leadership of the organization was inherited by Mohammed Yusuf's deputy, Abubakar Shekau, and likewise arguably the point at which the

---

[11] Note: other versions of this episode suggest that the Boko Haram group were specifically targeted after intelligence had been received that they were planning a major attack.

jihadist ambitions of the emerging leadership of Boko Haram began to define the ideological direction of what was now undeniably an armed militant group.

A note here on the personality and influence of Abubakar Shekau might perhaps be appropriate. Mohammed Yusuf had led the organization as a militant, but none the less largely passive organization focused on a millenarianist ideology and promoting a lifestyle of orthodox Islam. Abubakar Shekau, on the other hand, emerged immediately as a radical militant jihadist with a charismatic style of leadership and a sworn agenda to punish the Nigerian authorities for the killing of Mohammed Yusuf and generally to violently propagate a reversionist agenda of returning to the pure roots of Islam and punishing a nation for its venality and corruption, and its embrace of western influences.

There are very few undisputed facts available about who and what Abubakar Shekau is. His birth date is reckoned to be anywhere from 1972 to 1981, and the location of his birth has been named as either Niger or Shekau village in the Yobe State of northern Nigeria. He has been described as both complex and paradoxical, part gangster and part theologian, and he is known in certain contexts, and among other aliases, as *Darul Tawheed*. This translates as "specialist in tawheed", taweed being the Islamic concept of oneness of Allah.[12] The sense from this that Shekau is an Islamic scholar is perhaps misleading. Despite undeniable intelligence, and fluency in several languages, Abubakar Shekau remains only nominally educated.

Nonetheless, Abubakar Shekau espouses a radical form of Islam that Nigerian academic, Barkindo Atta of the School of African and Oriental Studies in London, describes as "a spill over from the Sunni-Salafi doctrine that the temporal proximity to Prophet Mohammad is associated with the truest form of Islam."[13]

In this case, temporal proximity implies simply a closer adherence to the original tenets of Islam, with Shekau, along with a number of other Salafi jihadists, freely advocating the use of violence, even violence against fellow Muslims and Salafi purists and activists who in one way or another deprecate violence or advocate any sort of participation in political processes and dialogue.

In this context, Boko Haram appears to ally itself with those Sunni-Salafi jihadists who are calling for and utilizing violence as a means of ensuring a reversion to the original forms of Islam, and the subsequent rejection of everything that can be deemed as *un-Islamic*. The foundations of Boko Haram's ideological propaganda, therefore, and the fundamentals of its recruitment message, and indeed its strategic and organizational structure, are all based on the principal of rejecting western influence, with the ultimate objective of building a society or caliphate based strictly on core Islamic values.[14] In this case, western influence is characterized primarily by the Nigerian federal government, but also elements within the state governments and the Islamic establishment that are deemed un-Islamic for one reason or another, or influenced by un-Islamic tendencies.

---

[12] *Profile of Nigeria's Boko Haram leader Abubakar Shekau.* BBC News. 22 June 2012.

[13] tonyblairfaithfoundation.org - Boko Haram: Ideology, Ethnicity and Identity

[14] Ibid.

An identifying characteristic of Boko Haram that differentiates it from more international jihadist organizations is the fact that, despite occasionally claiming to be linked into the international radical Islamic networks, Boko Haram has to date acted upon no wider regional or international objective than its fundamental opposition to the Nigerian government. There is evidence, however, that Boko Haram has received some logistical and technical assistance, and perhaps training from *al-Qaeda in the Islamic Maghreb* (AQIM), and other organizations, but so far claims that the movement is strategically linked to any transnational organization remain unproven.

Boko Haram has taken to using the same flag used by the Islamic State

There are, however, a number of anecdotal factors that will indicate at least a degree of logistical direction from larger and more sophisticated organizations, and an example of this is the recent use of improvised explosive devices (IED), and more specifically, vehicle bourn IEDs (VIED), and indeed the selection and training of suicide bombers, in particular female suicide bombers. On February 24, 2015, for example, a female suicide bomber, reported to be aged no more than seven, detonated an explosive device in a crowded market in the northern town of Potiskum, killing five and wounding dozens, followed later in the day by two further suicide bombers detonating explosive devices at bus terminus, the first in Potiskum and the second in Kano, this time collectively killing at least 27 people.

The first recorded Boko Haram suicide bombing was in fact recorded as early as 2011, which at the very least implies an aspirational link without outside organizations, and indeed, more recently, Boko Haram's printed and video propaganda material has come more closely to resemble that of the Islamic State (ISIS), which implies again at the very least an aspirational link, while reports of foreign looking and speaking militants visible in the ranks of Boko Haram again suggests the beginnings of a wider field of interest, and the possibility that Boko Haram is beginning to attract foreign jihadists.

Much of this information, however, originates from Nigerian intelligence sources, and there is naturally much to be much to be gained by the Nigerian federal government at least *claiming* that Boko Haram has morphed into an international organization, with increased financial and security aid from the international community being perhaps the most important inducement. Indeed, in the aftermath of the failed attempt to rescue hostages Chris McManus and Franco Lamolinara in March 2012, the details of which will be discussed later, Nigerian President Goodluck Jonathan began to place a far greater emphasis on the link between Boko Haram and international terrorism, to which the US State Department responded by obligingly placing Abubakar Shekau on the list of *Specially Designated Global Terrorist*, along with deputies Khalid al-Barnawi and Abubakar Adam Kambar.[15]

Al-Barnawi

Chapter 4: Boko Haram Tactics and Operations

Having eventually regained control of Maiduguri and other northern cities in the aftermath of the 2009 Boko Haram Uprising, police and security services embarked immediately on a brutal and bloody and punitive purge of the Boko Haram's members, and indeed anyone in the wider community suspected of being a supporter or a sympathizer. This forced those surviving members of the organization to flee the country, most either to Niger or Cameroon, although it

---

[15] Note: Khalid al-Barnawi, also known as Mohammed Usman, is an erstwhile high ranking member of Boko Haram and current leader of splinter faction Ansaru with known links to al-Shabab. Abubakar Adam Kambar was reported killed by Nigerian security forces prior to this designation.

was at that point that a handful of prominent members of Boko Haram were tracked to training camps in Algeria and Somalia, and according to the United Nations Security Council, a handful at least also received terror training in a Tuareg rebel camp in Mali.[16] What is clear, however, is that the hiatus that occurred for the remainder of 2009, and for the first half of 2010, were not idle months for Boko Haram, and towards the middle of 2010 members of the group began to reappear in Maiduguri, where they immediately began a campaign of assassinations.

Initially these attacks where quite unsophisticated and random, characterized by motorcycle gunmen targeting police checkpoints in hit-and-run operations in both Borno and Yobe states. Additional targets were local civic and political leaders who had been singled out for corruption, or for having informed on Boko Haram members during the purges of the year before. Individuals who had been apportioned homes and property formerly belonging to escaped Boko Haram members were also targeted and killed. Other operations included the September 2010 attack by about 50 gunmen on the central Bauchi prison, which resulted in the release of 721 prisoners.

On Christmas Eve 2010, the stakes were raised significantly when a series of bomb blasts targeted churches and a market in two districts of Jos, killing scores of people. These incidents were not initially attributed to Boko Haram, and were in fact attributed to another Nigerian militant organization, *Movement for the emancipation of the Niger Delta* (MEND), and indeed Henry Okah, a former leader of MEND, currently in custody in South Africa, still faces charges in Nigeria for one of those attacks.[17] The same was true on New Year's Eve when an open air fish market in Abuja was targeted, the second bomb attack in Abuja in three months, for which Boko Haram was not initially suspected.

Okah

[16] *What Is Boko Haram?* United States Institute of Peace, Special Report.

[17] *What Is Boko Haram?* United States Institute of Peace, Special Report.

An FBI assisted investigation ultimately revealed similarities in construction between the devices used in Jos and those in Abuja, at which point suspicion began to fall on Boko Haram. This, of course, was a significant tactical advance on the random assassinations and terrorist actions in and around Maiduguri, with the organization proving itself now able to extend its reach as far as Abuja, and moreover displaying a willingness to target civilians in high profile attacks aimed primarily at causing large numbers of civilian casualties.

There was also a paradoxical element of gangsterism associated with Boko Haram's activities at this time, with targets also being selected for the potential that they offered for extortion, kidnapping and simple robbery, which accounted in the early stages of the insurgency for much of Boko Haram's funding. Banks, cash in transit convoys and businesses were all becoming targets, justified as the spoils of war.

According to Abubakar Shekau himself, the killing of civilians "for the purpose of conquering and taking their money follows verses of the Qur'an." Here he is making reference to *ghanima*, or khums, meaning loosely the spoils of war but also taxation payable to a Sultan or Caliph from booty collected from non-believers in the aftermath of war. Thus, "we take from our enemies in the battle we fight in the name of Allah."[18]

On June 16, 2011, an enigmatic bomb attack was launched against police headquarters in Abuja when a car laden with explosives was driven into a secure compound in the wake of a convoy of senior officers in Abuja's government district. The vehicle was directed by security staff to the rear of the building where the explosives were detonated, killing the bomber himself and a single traffic policeman.

A great deal of speculation surrounded this attack. It is thought that the principal target was the Inspector General of Police whose convoy the bomber had followed into the compound, but it was not immediately clear whether the attack had been intended as a suicide bombing, or whether the driver had simply been delayed in Abuja traffic and was therefore unable to escape the blast himself. If, however, this had been an intended suicide bombing, then it would be the first such incident in the short history of the insurgency.

This question, however, was answered two months later in what was something of a coming of age attack for Boko Haram. On Friday, August 26, 2011, a vehicle crashed two security barriers and succeeded in ramming into the reception area of the main United Nations building in Abuja before detonating a quantity of explosives that killed the driver and a further 23 people in what would prove to be the most serious and successful terrorist attack in Nigeria to date. It was also the first Boko Haram operation that targeted an international institution, which represented a widening of its campaign. In the opinion of many intelligence analysts, it was through this attack that Boko Haram proved it was receiving international assistance.

The frequency, sophistication and brutality of Boko Haram attacks continued into 2012, escalating to the point where more attacks took place in the opening months of 2015 than had taken place in the whole of 2014. This is a clear indication of a massive escalation in Boko Haram's scope and reach, with the movement's funding network growing, and its access to

---

[18] CTC Sentinel – *Leadership Analysis of Boko Haram and Ansaru in Nigeria* By Jacob Zenn

sophisticated weaponry and operational intelligence exceeding in many respects the Nigerian security force's ability to respond. Civilian victims of Boko Haram totaled 6,347 during 2014, amounting to the largest number of civilian casualties of war recorded on the African continent that year.[19]

The largest and most deadly series of operation to date occurred between January 2-7, 2015, in a coordinated sequence of attacks against the town of Baga, in the extreme northeast of Nigeria, bordering Cameroon. The operation began on January 3 as Boko Haram elements overran a military base containing a *Multinational Joint Task Force* comprising troops and support personnel from Chad, Niger and Nigeria, which was followed by mass killings in and around the city that left possibly as many as 2,000 civilians dead, often in horrific circumstances.[20]

Responsibility for the episode was claimed by Boko Haram in a propaganda video that was released soon afterwards. In the video, Abubakar Shekau, in a lengthy rant, revealed large quantities of captured weaponry and equipment, threatened renewed attacks against targets in Cameroon and Chad, and condemned the actions of Nigerian president Goodluck Jonathan in joining solidarity marches in Paris supporting international outrage at the *Charlie Hebdo* killings.[21]

---

[19] The Guardian Friday 23 January 2015 - *Nigeria suffers highest number of civilian deaths in African war zones.*

[20] Note: These figures were proffered by Amnesty International, but have since been disputed by the Nigerian government, which claims a more accurate figure is 150. This, however, bearing in mind newsreel and satellite imagery, in very unlikely.

[21] Note: On 7 January 2015, two Islamist gunmen forced their way into and opened fire in the Paris headquarters of Charlie Hebdo, killing twelve and wounding eleven, four of them seriously.

Goodluck Jonathan

Indeed, the preceding weeks and months, a number of deadly attacks had been launched against both Chad and Cameroon, prompting each to weigh in with troops and support in what is in effect an internationalization of the insurgency. In December 2014, a Cameroonian soldier was killed in an attack that followed a series of earlier attacks against Cameroonian civilians, resulting collectively in an estimated 30 fatalities. Two days later, Cameroonian troops repelled four simultaneous Boko Haram raids on the towns of Makary, Amchide, Limani, Guirvidig, Waza and Achigachia, located in Cameroon's Far North Region. A number of militants were killed in a Cameroonian counterattack, with authorities estimating the number of Boko Haram members involved at over 1,000.

Similar threats and attacks have been launched against both Chad and Niger, with some suggestions that Boko Haram members have been active alongside AQIM in Mali, although in general it has been observed that Boko Haram attacks beyond Nigerian border have been confined primarily to the region defined as the old Bornu Caliphate which the movement seeks in some manner of form to replicate.

The extent of the insurgency within Nigeria, and its gradual internationalization, has prompted a great deal of discussion, handwringing and international anxiety. However, only limited military and intelligence assistance to Nigeria began to accrue from a number of sources, most notably the United States. America has provided to date a small amount of financial and counter-terrorism assistance under the umbrella of the Anti-terrorism Assistance Program and the Trans-Sahara Counterterrorism Partnership.[22] However, it is perhaps also worth noting that former U.S. Ambassador to Nigeria, John Campbell, who is now a Council on Foreign Relations senior fellow for Africa policy studies, has on frequent occasions warned the White House to resist the temptation to characterize Boko Haram as simply another foe in the global war on terrorism, since the group's grievances have been to date, and fundamentally remain, primarily local.[23] According to Campbell, "The Boko Haram insurgency is a direct result of chronic poor governance by Nigeria's federal and state governments, the political marginalization of northeastern Nigeria, and the region's accelerating impoverishment. Rather than fighting the militant group solely through military force, the U.S. and Nigerian governments must work together to redress the alienation of Nigeria's Muslims."[24]

---

[22] http://www.state.gov/r/pa/prs/ps/2014/05/226072.htm

[23] Council on Foreign Relations, November 2014 – *U.S. Policy to Counter Nigeria's Boko Haram.*

[24] Council on Foreign Relations, November 2014 – *U.S. Policy to Counter Nigeria's Boko Haram.*

Campbell

Campbell advised that a more viable strategy for Washington to pursue in Nigeria would be to leverage what influence it had to ensure free, fair and credible elections in Nigeria in 2015, and for the government of Nigeria to curb the blatant human rights abuses that have so far characterized the official Nigerian response to the insurgency, and to meet the needs of refugees and persons internally displaced by the ongoing fighting in the northeast.

This, however, despite being extremely sage advice in the context of avoiding direct engagement, and in quantifying the insurgency as less an international terrorist threat and more a manifestation of understandable grievances within a tottering system, seems also to be somewhat forlorn when considering the complete inability of the Nigerian security services to adequately come to grips with the insurgency, and its subsequent tendency to lash out in all directions, targeting the wider civilian population in a misdirected and largely ineffective counter-insurgency (COIN) operation.

Chapter 5: The Nigerian Counter-Insurgency Response

The quality of an army, or indeed any armed force, can only really be quantified in relation to the quality of its enemy, and perhaps the most interesting ramification of the Boko Haram insurgency has been the way in which it has demonstrated tremendous deficiencies in the ability of Nigerian military to respond to what really amounts to a very limited regional insurgency, and one that enjoys only very limited mainstream popular support.

From its origins as a battalion of the Royal West African Frontier Force, the Nigerian armed forces have evolved very much according to British and Commonwealth traditions, with a majority of senior officers at independence being Sandhurst trained and handpicked by the British themselves. Thus, they are supposed to represent not only the very cream of Nigerian manpower but also characterize the strengths of British military training and tradition, and, perhaps most importantly, to ensure to the greatest extent possible that the armed forces of a newly independent British colony would pose the lowest risk possible of indiscipline.

The British, therefore, invested an inordinate amount of time and treasure into training and arming the new Nigerian army, which ultimately suffered the same failing as the country as a whole: ethnic divisions and rivalries that ultimately tore the force apart. One of the first compromises made was to configure the various regiments and battalions along ethnic lines in the aftermath of the first 1966 coup, and to deploy them more or less according to the delineations of their home regions.

The first major test of independent Nigerian military capability was the civil war of 1967-70, which revealed a great deal of form and procedure, but much tactical dilettantism as well, alongside clear evidence of a tendency towards ethnic equalization and a high tolerance of human rights abuses. Federal forces won that contest less as a consequence military prowess than its overwhelming logistical advantage occasioned by almost universal international political support, and a great effort on the part of the British to ensure that the federation that they had created survived.

The next major military challenge for Nigeria came with its majority involvement in the Economic Community of West African States (ECOWAS) peacekeeping efforts in Liberia and Sierra Leone, under the aegis of the Economic Community of West African States Monitoring Group (ECOMOG), which devolved into a blatantly corrupt scramble to seize its share of the natural and economic spoils of two nations in absolute crisis. Indeed, the popular local interpretation of the acronym ECOMOG became "Every Car or Moving Object Gone."

It therefore comes as no particular surprise that the armed forces of Nigeria have manifestly failed to come to grips with Boko Haram. Perhaps the most telling hint of Nigeria's lack of military preparedness or integrity comes from the result of the failed hostage rescue attempt to secure the freedom of British and Italian hostages Chris McManus and Franco Lamolinara. The operation, undertaken by the British Special Boat Service, in cooperation with unspecified Nigerian armed force units, attempted in March 2012 to storm a house in the northern city of Sokoto in the extreme northwest of Nigeria. They were hoping to free the hostages after reports of their imminent movement and killing were intercepted by British intelligence agencies. The attempt, undertaken in broad daylight, failed, and the two hostages, alongside two militants, were killed.

Anecdotal reports suggest that much of the failure of the operation had to do with the diplomatic necessity of British Special Forces cooperating with the Nigerians, combined with leaking of information and prior warning being given to the militants.[25] While this remains anecdotal, and in the absence of a tactical analysis of the operation, the facts of its failure will likely remain unknown for some time to come, but the deficiencies of the Nigerian COIN response have been fairly well documented.

A fundamental principal of counter-insurgency is the question of "hearts and minds," which was established as part of the Briggs Plan in Malaya during the Malayan Uprising of 1948-60, during which the earliest precepts of dealing with popular uprisings and 'People's War' were evolved. These were then collected and refined in various campaigns ranging from the Mau Mau Uprising at more or less the same time to the Portuguese colonial wars in Africa and the Rhodesian and South African wars of liberation.

The Boko Haram insurgency conforms to the classic definition of asymmetric warfare, meaning there are two opposing forces with vastly different military capabilities. One (for the most part) represents the state in a conventional configuration, and the second represents the militant expression of a popular movement, usually responding to deep-seated discontent leveled against the government. This is broadly the case in northern Nigeria. The Nigerian method of winning hearts and minds, as with the case of many conventional responses to popular movements, seeks to avoid recognition of authentic political grievance, removing, therefore, from its mandate any obligation towards social improvement and instead relying on a reapplication of terror in order to terrorize the terrorists.

In a September 2014 report entitled "Welcome to Hellfire," Amnesty International drew attention to systematic human rights abuses being perpetrated by the Nigerian armed forces in pursuit of Operation Flush, a deeply questionable counter-insurgency operation implemented in 2009 as the Boko Haram operational profile began to include attacks against security forces, schools, churches and civilians. Initially, a Joint Task Force (JTF) was established, comprising personnel from all of the various security services. This operated under a state of emergency that had been declared in 15 northern Local Government Areas (LGAs) by President Goodluck Jonathan, initially in January 2012, and extended in May 2013 to include Adamaw, Borno and Yobe states. This State of Emergency has since been extended twice.

In 2013, the JTF was dissolved and operational command of security operations was handed over to the Army Chief of Staff, at which point a tactical shift saw the formation and deployment of a Civilian Joint Task Force (CJTF). The CJTF is essentially a state-sponsored civilian militia with powers to arrest suspected Boko Haram members or sympathizers. And of course, under wide ranging emergency laws, the security forces themselves enjoy sweeping powers to arrest and detain anyone suspected of terror related offences.

---

[25] Note: Militants in this instance belonged to a suggested splinter group of Boko Haram, *Ansaru*, or *Jamā'atu Anṣāril Muslimīna fī Bilādis Sūdān* (Vanguard for the Protection of Muslims in Black Lands)

The result of all of this has been an effective and officially sanctioned reign of terror as mobs of sparsely trained (if at all) local youth, empowered by almost total impunity, descend on local communities with arbitrary powers to select and interrogate any individuals who upon any basis at all might be deemed members of, sympathetic to, or in some way associated with Boko Haram. Mass arrests, beatings, torture and killings have both been reported and recorded, with a great deal of graphic video and photographic evidence surfacing that implicates state security agents in a number of horrific and blatant human rights abuses, many of which constitute de facto war crimes. Perhaps the most shocking evidence has been a variety of amateur videos taken of the extra-judicial killing of a number of civilians whose throats were individually cut before being tossed into a mass grave by elements of the Nigerian military assisted by members of the CJTF.

Although difficult to deny, the Nigerian government has nonetheless attempted to do so. The claim has been made that the executions were perpetrated by members of Boko Haram masquerading as Nigerian soldiers, which has indeed taken place on several occasions, but in this case there is clear evidence on video of the incident that proves that this was not so. Perhaps the most compelling is the result of an analysis of visible rifle markings that identify a weapon in the possession of a soldier as belonging to a specific Nigerian battalion.

Much of this has been revealed by a handful of Western media outlets, including PBS *Frontline* and the British Channel 4 *Dispatches,* each of which produced revealing and deeply disturbing documentaries illustrating, not only the Nigerian security services, in particular the police and army, but also the CJTF implicated in random and widespread human rights abuses, running the gamut of beatings, arbitrary arrest and detention, mass killings and public executions. Alongside this was testimony taken from a number of former members and currently serving members of the CJTF confirming mass atrocities against civilians, which also revealed the ad hoc nature and extreme brutality exercised by what is in effect an undisciplined mob of largely unemployed and disaffected teenagers, crudely armed, empowered and acting with almost absolute impunity.

Military operations documented by Amnesty International and various other sources describe a pattern of mass arrests and screenings of people, many identifiable as children, in towns and villages, typically as a consequence of fairly random identification, and usually thereafter involving beatings and other violent abuse. Those detained as suspected members of Boko Haram are often held incommunicado in local or smaller military camps without access to family or legal representation for long periods. Torture and other ill-treatment by the soldiers has been routine – either at the time of, or immediately after arrest, or while detained – often to punish them for their alleged links with Boko Haram, and indeed large numbers of people have simply disappeared, with many later turning up dead.

Needless to say, there has been no serious attempt on the part of the Nigerian authorities to investigate or act upon allegations brought against the military and police by, in particular, Amnesty International. When contacted for comment upon the release of the Channel 4 documentary *Nigeria's Hidden War,* the Nigerian High Commissioner in London dismissed purported cases of human rights abuses and war crimes. He asserted "nothing of the sort is being perpetrated in Nigeria. This is because there has to be a war before you talk about war crimes. What is happening ...is an effort ...to stamp out insurgency...[Where] possible collateral damage could be experienced. The Nigerian Government ... is a signatory to many international human rights instruments, ... is doing everything possible within the ambit of law... [The] Government ... or its agencies cannot be said to be targeting unprotected civilians as a matter of policy."[26]

More focused Amnesty International attempts to raise concerns with the Nigerian government and military have resulted in a tacit acceptance of mass arrests and torture as a broad strategy, but rationalizing it as means justifying ends: "It's a natural reaction by the army to cordon off an area to search when we don't get adequate information about particular acts... We also have challenges in investigating or detecting the truth. So we have to make do with the crude method we have. These extra measures are necessary for the context we operate in."[27]

In August 2014, the office of the National Security Officer in Nigeria wrote to Amnesty International and conceded, "Our security and law enforcement agencies are committed to abiding by the Geneva Conventions and all standard operating procedures designed to maximize the protection of civilians when fighting an armed and hidden insurgency, which blends in with the local population. That said, however, there have indeed been abuses committed where our security and law enforcement operatives failed to abide by those important standards. We are however determined to do better and happily with each passing day we are doing better."[28]

Those claims aside, the weight of anecdotal evidence alone is sufficiently compelling to conclude that a violent and indiscriminate campaign was, and in many instances still is, being waged in the northeast of Nigeria in an attempt to stamp out popular support for the Boko Haram movement.

Chapter 6: The International Response

It is interesting to note that it was in the immediate aftermath of Chibok kidnappings that calls for some sort of an international intervention were most loudly spoken, and most universally acknowledged. In May 2014, a month after the kidnappings, a summit meeting between French and affected African heads of state was held in Paris to explore ways and means of coordinating a campaign against Boko Haram. A great deal of people articulated the international threat and called for action. One of the most notable was Senator John McCain, who called for an American military operation to rescue the kidnapped girls, but ultimately there remains great international reluctance to actively intervene against Boko Haram.[29]

---

[26] *channel4.com* - Nigeria's Hidden War: Channel 4 Dispatches. August 18 2014

[27] Amnesty International's meeting with senior military officers at Defense headquarters in Abuja, 31 July 2013.
[28] Letter to Amnesty International from the Office of the National Security Adviser, 7 August 2014.

[29] McCain's call was based on humanitarian and not strategic rationale.

A picture of damage done to the school where the girls were kidnapped

A picture of some of the girls' parents crying after the kidnapping

Nigeria lies within what might be regarded as the British sphere of influence, given that it is a former British colony and an Anglophone country, but the likelihood of an international response, if any, would in all probability originate in France. West Africa, broadly speaking, exists within the French sphere of interest more than it does any other colonizing power. French defense agreements with a majority of her ex-colonies have seen French military interventions in

Gabon, Chad, CAR, Comoros, Zaire, Djibouti, Republic of Congo and more recently in Côte-d'Ivoire, Libya and Mali. However, France did not directly interfere in the Biafran War of 1967-70, but likewise neither did Britain, and the only significant intervention by Britain in the region since then has been Operation Barras, which was a special force operation that took place in Sierra Leone on September 10, 2000 to release five British soldiers of the Royal Irish Regiment who had been held by a local militia group. American intervention, if held back during the depth of the Rwandan, Liberian and Sierra Leonean crisis, is unlikely to be forthcoming in Nigeria, in particular in the aftermath of the disastrous intervention in Somalia.

The likelihood, therefore, of any direct outside military action in Nigeria to confront Boko Haram is extremely remote. The integrity of the Nigerian state is not at risk, and although there is very little practical hope that the Nigerian security forces will ever regain full control over what is traditionally a wild and lawless region, there is also no risk of an imminent coup d'état, or any other such hazard to the central government.

There is also the question of Nigeria's almost mind-numbing levels of corruption and the obvious excesses in its counter-insurgency efforts, as demonstrated by the unpalatable evidence of extreme human rights abuses being perpetrated against the civilian population of the north. Some of these have been anecdotally classified as war crimes, which make any international dealings with Nigeria diplomatically tricky to say the very least.

Part of this has to do with the fact that Boko Haram's creed continues to focus locally, as well as the fact that the organization's opposition against the Nigerian government is understandable in the sense that the Nigerian forces have committed atrocities. In fact, some of the worst excesses of violence perpetrated by Boko Haram are not that much worse than the worst excesses of the security establishment in responding to the crisis. Thus, the primary diplomatic challenge must be for Western governments to first bolster the democratic institutions of Nigeria, assist with the eradication of corruption, and help professionalize the military by attempting to build the necessary trust and empathy between them and the population that they purport to defend.

Chapter 7: Uncertain Future

According to former U.S. Ambassador to Nigeria, John Campbell, Boko Haram poses no direct security threat to the U.S. homeland, but its attacks on Nigeria, and Abuja's response that is characterized by extensive human-rights violations, does challenge American interests in Africa.[30] There exists a significant risk that if Boko Haram is actively pursued with the same arsenal of political, financial and military options being deployed against such organizations and ISIS, al-Qaeda, al-Shebaba and AQIM, Boko Haram will by association be elevated to that status and will begin to attract the interest, recruitment and funding of international jihadists. In a sense, this would create the very problem that the international community seeks to avoid. At the same time, it's probably safe to assume some elements of Boko Haram are ambitious enough to seek associations with foreign terror franchises to boost their own image internationally.

[30] International Business Times January 18 2015 – *Boko Haram: United States Intervention In Nigeria Is Complicated, Officials Say.*

There are no definitive studies available detailing the organization and leadership structure of Boko Haram, which more than anything else underlines the shadowy nature of the movement and its leadership. It is recognized, however, that as the organization has matured in the five or six years since it has been operational, complex leadership structures have evolved along the lines of an independent cell structure under the broad umbrella leadership of a *Shura Council*, headed, nominally at least, by Abubakar Shekau. That said, there is by no means unanimity in intelligence or academic circles that he is either the only or the absolute leader of the group.[31]

According to U.S. Congressional research, the core group of Boko Haram numbers in the hundreds rather than the thousands, with a much wider field of informal support available primarily within the Kanuri tribal group. Abubakar Shekau belongs to this group, which geographically overlaps the four corners region of Nigeria, Niger, Chad and Cameroon. This is the region which also defines, incidentally, more or less the borders of the old Bornu/Sokoto Caliphates which Boko Haram, at least ideologically, is committed to bringing back.

Even the within the Shura Council itself, the leadership is disperse and remote, offering a degree of anonymity but also leading to a fractured decision making process and the tendency for confusion and miscommunication. Individual members of the Shura Council rarely meet, instead communicating through human liaison and cell phones, and in this way controlling a system of individual cells that are responsible for different roles and functions within the organization, as well as specific geographic areas. For example, certain cells specialize in and are responsible for the racketeering aspects of the group's activities, including the bank and cash in transit robberies, money laundering and the acquisition of vehicles and general equipment. Others are responsible for providing intelligence services, including the selection and research of targets and modes of operation, and yet others are more combat oriented, others more technical. There are, for example, bomb makers, as well as those for funding cells, propaganda and media, external relations and welfare/medical. The latter is responsible for the care of wives and families of deceased members and relatives of suicide bombers.[32]

There are reported to be at least 30 individual cells, each overseen and commanded by a different council member, with overall decisions made within the council. On occasion, there's a propensity for Abubakar Shekau to act independently and autonomously, which again adds to the tendency towards miscommunication and division. In essence, any definitive statement issued by the organization might not be wholly representative of group opinion or determination.[33]

It would appear also that Abubakar Shekau maintains very little contact with the operative structures of Boko Haram, dealing instead with only a handful of select cell leaders. This leads to a degree of operational unpredictability, but it also makes it much more difficult to negotiate with a group that appears to have many individual heads, each to some degree independent of the other.

---

[31] Note: *Shura* is an Arabic word implying inclusive consultation. The Quran, and indeed Muhammad himself, encourage all Muslims to decide their affairs in consultation with those affected by any decision. A Shura Council, therefore, is a standard organizational/administrative body in the Islamic world, with Shura Councils, or consultative councils, existing in one form or another in most predominantly Islamic countries.

[32] Sahara Reporters July 15 2012 - *Boko Haram Reportedly Has Complex Organizational Structure.*

[33] Walker, Andrew. *United States Institute of Peace*, June 2012, *What is Boko Haram?*

It is inevitable, therefore, that the organization would be subject to internal divisions, and in key policy aspects, would be seen to be pulling in different directions. Like other sectarian Muslim groups, its ideological premise has compelled Boko Haram to lash out frequently at fellow Muslims. In fact, a majority of Boko Haram's victims have been northern Nigerian Muslims, with the movement even targeting those within its own membership and support base in order to settle internal factionalism and disagreements.[34]

It might perhaps be instructive in concluding an examination of the Boko Haram leadership to dwell briefly on the nature of these internal divisions, for they determine to a significant extent the general ambiguity of the organization, and indeed the tendency towards internationalization as the movement itself matures away from its established, founding leadership.

Perhaps the most extreme example of internal contradiction occurred in January 2012, when a group claiming to be a moderate breakaway faction of Boko Haram released a video tape to the Nigerian Television Authority offering terms of negotiation. Four days later, men claiming to be Boko Haram publicly beheaded six people in Maiduguri. Indeed, according to the U.S. Institute of Peace, when Boko Haram kills their own, they behead them, and reports of beheadings seem to go up when there are talks of negotiation.[35]

Internal divisions within the movement are also premised to some extent on ethnic lines. The Boko Haram base of operations spreads over a wide geographic area, and differing ethnic groups are not only targeted by the group but also inducted. This means the ethnic composition of the upper ranks and leadership begins to dilute. The Kanuri ethnic group that makes up the majority within Boko Haram occupies a limited geographic area in the northeast of Nigeria, and it is significantly outnumbered within the wider region of Islamic influence in northern Nigeria by the Hausa/Fulani group. Both groups practices Islam in different ways, and on the wider religious/political stage in Nigeria, the Hausa/Fulani are significantly more influential. According to one report from STRATFOR Global Intelligence, "As Boko Haram attacks began to kill more Hausa-Fulani, a backlash among western Nigerian Muslims has been mounting, particularly in Kano, Nigeria's second largest city and the country's northern commercial hub."[36]

Perhaps the most significant impact of internal division and leadership contradictions within Boko Haram is the potential ideological merger between Boko Haram and the wider diaspora of Islamic jihadist organizations. In a highly detailed study of the Boko Haram leadership by Jacob Zenn, a respected African and Eurasian Affairs analyst, the author details a number of Mohammed Yusuf's "disciples," including Abubakar Shekau, each with differing views on the strategic and ideological direction of the movement and each tending to pull in different directions. One such member is Mamman Nur, who masterminded the 2011 UN bombing in Abuja, and who, also known as Abu Usmatul al-Ansari, was a founder member of Ansaru. Nur is a Cameroonian with significant contacts to international terrorist organizations such as AQIM,

---

[34] U.S. House of Representatives Committee on Homeland Security September 13, 2013 - BOKO HARAM: A Growing Threat to the U.S. Homeland.

[35] *Ibid.*

[36] *Ibid.*

al-Shabaab, MUJAO, al-Qaeda Central, and other militant groups in Africa. What is interesting about him is the fact that he fled Nigeria in the aftermath of the 2009 uprising in the direction of East Africa, finding refuge and ultimately training and ideological direction from al- Shabaab in Somalia. When he returned, he was highly motivated to regionalize the Boko Haram agenda.[37]

Nur

Mention has already been made of Khalid al-Barnawi and Abubakar Adam Kambar (the latter of whom is probably dead), each of which exerted a strong influence towards regionalization and internationalization of the Boko Haram insurgency. This is suggestive of other strong influences within the organization, and perhaps to a degree its future direction. As a result, when trying to chart its future course, the question to be answered is one of leadership, because regardless of its rapid advances in scope and capability, Boko Haram remains proscribed by the limitations of its current leadership. According to Jacob Zenn, "Boko Haram's future trajectory may depend on Mamman Nur. Due to Nur's ideological influence on Ansaru and operational connections to AQIM, al-Shabab and the late Kambar, Nur may be the "Boko Haram" leader communicating with AQIM, al-Shabab, al-Qa'ida in the Arabian Peninsula (AQAP), the Islamic Movement of Uzbekistan (IMU) in Pakistan and other al-Qa'ida affiliates."[38]

Currently, it is recognized that Boko Haram is an affiliate of al-Qaeda, and associated on some level with al- Shabaab, which is itself more closely associated with al-Qaeda. However, all of those links, along with Boko Haram's associations with militant organizations in North Africa, remain imperfectly understood, suggesting that a full association is still off in the distance rather than already here. The future leadership question is vexed, however. Shekau remains a divisive leader, but he enjoys legitimacy based on his ethnic origins, his grassroots support, and his credentials as Mohammed Yusuf's second-in-command. Any leadership change would likely see

---

[37] Note: it ought not to be assumed from this that Abubakar Shekau lacks interest in being absorbed into a foreign jihadist franchise, or indeed franchising Boko Haram itself. There simply appears to be significant limitations to Shekau's leadership ability, notwithstanding his apparent firm grip on the organization at present. There is evidence that Shekau is not taken seriously outside of Nigeria, and there may be a reluctance on the part of outside organizations to invest in a movement that is led by an individual displaying evidence of instability and erratic leadership, which may well changed at some point in the future when control of the organization is passed on.

[38] CTC Sentinel - *Leadership Analysis of Boko Haram and Ansaru in Nigeria*, by Jacob Zenn

Khalid al-Barnawi assuming operational control of Boko Haram and Mamman Nur assuming ideological control, at which point, thanks to the latter's connections but also to the increasingly robust tactical capability of the organization, is a scenario to be taken very seriously indeed.

Indeed, whatever limitations there might be on the ideological proliferation of Boko Haram, what is inescapable is that it is growing in tactical capability and is gradually acquiring an impressive arsenal of military equipment despite the localized success claimed against it by the Nigerian security services. The recent Libyan conflict has made available military hardware that has the potential to significantly amplify the current level of threat. Among these are a number of variants of SA-7B MANPAD missile systems, which could be used to target both civilian and military aircraft. In addition, the organization is now in a position to deploy between 500 and 1,000 militants in any ground operation, supported by captured ordnance including 81mm mortars and a variety of armored vehicles and armored troop carriers along with a fleet of converted civilian vehicles.

Thus, in every respect, Boko Haram is a force both to be recognized and feared, and while it lacks the capability at the moment to fatally compromise the existing government in Abuja, it definitely retains the capacity to increase insecurity in the north. It may even be possible for the group to carve out its desired caliphate and hold territory in an increasing tenuous and lawless region of Africa. All the while, even though there is still no direct evidence that Boko Haram has morphed into an international terrorist organization, it now possesses the ability and a stated interest in attacking Western interests, which would simply require a modest leadership and ideological realignment to achieve.

Printed in Great Britain
by Amazon